Language Readers

Level 2
Book F
Units 31–36

Jane Fell Greene
Judy Fell Woods

ISBN 1-57035-440-5
ISBN 1-57035-276-3 Set

Text layout and design by Kimberly Harris
Cover design by Becky Malone
Cover Image © 2000 by Digital Vision Ltd.
Illustrated by Peggy Ranson

This product is in compliance with AB2519 California State
Adoption revision requirements.

Printed in the United States of America

Published and Distributed by

SOPRIS
WEST

4093 Specialty Place • Longmont, CO 80504 • (303) 651-2829
www.sopriswest.com

Contents

COUNT US OUT

UNIT 31

Phonology/Orthography Concepts

- The diphthongs **ow** and **ou** both represent the phoneme in **now**.
  - Use **ow** at the end of a syllable (**now**, **cow**, **how**); or in the mid-position when **ow** is followed by **-n**, **-l**, or **-er**.
  - Use **ou** in the mid-position of a syllable (unless **ou** is followed by **-n**, **-l**, or **-er**).

Vocabulary

about	found	pounding	*he'd*
allowed	fowl	proud	*it'd*
around	Frogtown	shouting	*I'd*
blouse	how	sound	*I've*
bound	loud	town	*she'd*
bow	mound	trout	*they'd*
count	mouth	vowel	*they've*
counted	out	without	*we'd*
down	plow		*we've*
downtown	pound		*you'd*
			you've

2

COUNT US OUT

Story Summary:

Kim's mom has gone to bed with a terrible headache. Kim is not allowed to walk downtown alone, so she convinces Pat to go with her to buy aspirin for her mother. Pat and Kim have to walk through Frogtown, a rough part of town, and are bullied by some older girls who try to frighten them.

When Kim's mother came home from school, she said, "Kim, I'd like to, but I can't help you with your science project today. My head is pounding."

While her mother went into her room to rest, Kim tried not to make a sound. Her mother had gone through a lot this year.

Mrs. Chung had been a teacher for twenty years. She adored her students. But this year, there were people in her class who made things terrible for everybody.

Kim remembered what her mom said about three girls who took something that belonged to someone else. And how some boys had spoken so disrespectfully to Mrs. Chung and the principal that they couldn't even come back around school for a week.

"I'd like to tell them what they are doing to my mother," Kim thought.

Later, Pat came by, shouting about her math test. "Wouldn't you like to see what I got? A 'B'! Haven't I gotten smart since Sid started helping me?" Pat was thrilled.

"I wish you'd go downtown with me," said Kim. "I am not allowed to go alone, but I'd like to get some aspirin for Mother. Those kids in her class are making her sick again. Wouldn't you like to ask them why they act the way they do?" Kim and her mom only had each other, and Kim hated to see her mother so miserable.

"We'd have to hurry," Pat responded. "I have to be home by about six. Dad has a meeting, so I have to baby-sit Trish."

Kim's mother didn't let her go downtown alone, since she had to go through Frogtown. Frogtown wasn't a very safe place after dark. But the two girls had plenty of time to get to the store and be back home before then.

"I'd counted on Mom helping me with my science project," Kim said. "I shouldn't have waited until the last minute, but I just haven't gotten started on it."

When they got to Main Street, they saw some ninth grade girls from Mrs. Chung's class standing on the corner. "How come your mother let you come down around Frogtown, little Chung?" the big one asked.

Shantel Jefferson had on a red blouse and lots of makeup. She had a loud mouth and was never without her pals. Kim and Pat hurried, trying to avoid Shantel's gang.

"They think they are grown-up. They think other kids have to bow down to them. But they'd better count us out. Kids like that aren't really grown-up," remarked Pat.

One girl grabbed Kim. They wouldn't let Pat and Kim pass. "Aren't you the little Chung? How'd you like to come with us?" they teased. "You think since your mom is a teacher, you are a hotshot, don't you?"

"That's not so," Pat responded. "You don't even know Kim!" Pat Marks had a hot temper, but Kim was shy. Kim nudged Pat, trying to signal her to be quiet.

"Please," Kim begged Shantel. "My mother is sick. I need to get back home to help her. I won't say anything. I promise."

"You can't trust them," said one of the girls. "They'd tell in a minute. You'd better keep them here with us, Shantel."

Kim was terrified. Even Pat was afraid. Why hadn't they listened to their parents? How could they be so foolish? There was a good reason they were not permitted to go downtown alone.

When Kim eyed a black car, she whispered, "Pat, isn't that your dad?"

Pat shouted, "Dad! Dad! Stop!" Even though Pat realized that there would be punishment from Mr. Marks, she also understood that it would be better than staying on the corner with Shantel's gang.

Shantel and her friends scattered. "They aren't so brave, are they?" Pat said.

The two hurried into Pat's dad's car.

Back at Kim's, Mr. Marks and Mrs. Chung sat down together. "Our girls intended well," said Mr. Marks. "But they weren't thinking clearly. They shouldn't have gone. Period."

"You're right, Herbert," Mrs. Chung replied. "I was about to burst with pride when I heard how Kim went out for the aspirin. I am proud of her. But I don't want her to do it again!"

"It's OK, Mom," Kim embraced her mother. I won't ever go downtown alone again. I promise!"

Teacher/Parent Pages

Use the following questions to stimulate language growth, imagination, conceptual relationships, and higher-level thinking skills. These activities will encourage conversation and help develop language skills. Students must know that their ideas are important and that their questions will be heard. Have fun and accept all reasonable answers while praising and encouraging questioning from the students.

Vocabulary Expansion

Describe and define these words and phrases:

good intentions	terrorize	science project
burst with pride	count us out	wait until the last minute
hotshot	bow down to	hang out
hot temper	makeup	expel
tell in a minute	gang	disrespectful

Language Expansion Activities

1. Act out the part of the story in which the ninth grade girls were teasing and scaring Kim and Pat. Why do you think the older girls were teasing them so badly? What kinds of things did they probably say?

2. Make a list of the ways in which students disrupt the class and make it hard for teachers to do their jobs. What can be done about it? If you were the principal, what new rules would you establish in your own school? Why? Make a poster listing them. Share it with your principal.

Language Expansion Questions

1. Why couldn't Mrs. Chung help Kim with her science project?

2. What did Kim decide to do for her mom? Why wasn't that a wise thing for her to do? Have you ever done anything against your parent(s)' wishes? What happened as a result of your actions?

3. Retell the events of the story in your own words.

4. Can you remember a time when you thought you were doing something good that turned out to be bad? Explain how something can be good and bad at the same time.

5. Why were Kim and Pat afraid of Shantel and her gang? Would you be afraid of them?

6. Create a new ending for the story. Imagine that Pat's dad hadn't been driving by in his car.

7. Kim had counted on her mom helping her with her science project, but she waited until the day before it was due to tell her. Why was this a bad decision on Kim's part? Have you ever waited until the last minute to do a project for school? Why is this a foolish way to handle an assignment?

8. Shantel and her gang called Kim "little Chung." Why? Has anybody ever called you names you didn't like? What did you do?

9. Some people have loud mouths. They brag. They tease and taunt others. They use bad language. Why do they behave that way? What does the saying "Shallow brooks are noisy" mean?

10. Decide whether the girls were treated fairly by their parents. Do you think they should have been punished?

THANKSGIVING

UNIT 31

Phonology/Orthography Concepts

- The diphthongs **ow** and **ou** both represent the phoneme in **now**.
  - Use **ow** at the end of a syllable (**now**, **cow**, **how**); or in the mid-position when **ow** is followed by **-n**, **-l**, or **-er**.
  - Use **ou** in the mid-position of a syllable (unless **ou** is followed by **-n**, **-l**, or **-er**).

Vocabulary

about	found	pounding	*he'd*
allowed	fowl	proud	*it'd*
around	Frogtown	shouting	*I'd*
blouse	how	sound	*I've*
bound	loud	town	*she'd*
bow	mound	trout	*they'd*
count	mouth	vowel	*they've*
counted	out	without	*we'd*
down	plow		*we've*
downtown	pound		*you'd*
			you've

THANKSGIVING

Story Summary:

Gram and Gramps come for a Thanksgiving visit. Pat's father invites the North family to join them for the holiday. Gram and Mrs. North help Herbert cook the turkey. Gramps doesn't feel well, and takes a nap right after dinner.

"Dad, it's so good to hear your voice!" said Herbert Marks. "The girls and I will come to pick up you and Mom." The three of them bundled up and hopped into the car.

When they got back home, Pat said, "Gramps, don't you want to stop smoking? Gram, can't we get him to quit?"

"I wish he'd quit," said Gram, "but after fifty years, it's hard to stop."

"Leave your grandfather alone," said Herbert. "Mom, you come into the kitchen with me. I need your advice on this twenty-pound fowl we got for tomorrow. This will be our best Thanksgiving ever!"

"Did Dad tell you that Sid and Hi are going to join us for Thanksgiving dinner?" asked Trish, who was seven.

"And Mrs. North. She's the best lady. And Hi can play video games with me, can't he, Pat?"

"Gramps, tell us about how you'd plow the fields with a mule when you were a little boy. And tell us about how Star and the piglets are doing. I couldn't wait for you to come and tell me a story!" Trish adored her grandfather.

"I don't think I'd better. I need to take a little rest for an hour or so," Gramps said.

As Gramps went up the stairs, Herbert Marks looked at his mother. "What is the matter? Isn't he feeling up to par? He's never refused Trish anything in his life!"

"We shouldn't have come. He hasn't felt well," Gram said. "But he wouldn't give up Thanksgiving for anything."

"Isn't he going to eat turkey with us tomorrow?" Trish asked. "And doesn't he want to see my reading test on vowel sounds? I got 94! Isn't that good, Gram?"

Pat came into the kitchen to give Dad and Gram a hand. They were chopping bread for the dressing. It wasn't as much fun without Gramps around. He was always the one who told the jokes. He was the one who made Thanksgiving such fun for everybody else.

The next morning, Gramps came down early. "A long, sound sleep is bound to cure whatever ails you!" he declared.

When they all sat down at the dinner table, Mrs. North said, "We have lots to rejoice about. Good things have happened to Hi and Sid and me this year."

Herbert said, "I propose a toast: May we have health, wealth, and long lives."

As they clinked their goblets, the others responded, "Hear! Hear!"

"I get the rest of the cranberry bread after everybody else has some!" declared Trish. They could sit around the dinner table for three hours while Trish ate nothing but bread. Gram said she was a picky eater.

Sid and Pat said they would like to go to Sam's after they'd attacked the mound of dishes. Their class was having a party.

Trish thought to herself, "Goody! Won't I be lucky! I get Gramps to myself!" But Gramps went to bed before six. He said he just didn't feel well.

When Trish turned on the TV to play video

games with Hi, Gram asked her to keep the sound down low.

That evening, Herbert and Mrs. North chatted with Gram. They spoke about Lake School. "The school that Trish and Hi attended had a fire in September," Herbert explained. "Mr. Grunch, one of the town's residents, found out about the fire and donated his stocks to rebuild the school. Their playground was rebuilt, too. By the beginning of October, the children had returned to school."

"It was amazing," Mrs. North said. "It's not fair to judge people. No one would have thought Mr. Grunch would be the one to come through! But he did! And we are grateful!"

After the Norths had left, Herbert and his

mother sat beside the fireplace for a last cup of coffee. "He has toiled for so many years," Gram said, "and he can't seem to stop. Maybe you can help me get him to the doctor, Herbert."

Trish came down for one last kiss. "I don't think it was really Thanksgiving today, Daddy," she said. "I didn't feel like rejoicing. Couldn't we try to have it again tomorrow?"

Herbert picked Trish up to tuck her in bed and read her a story. But while he was reading *Black Beauty*, the thing he was thinking of was his father.

Teacher/Parent Pages

Use the following questions to stimulate language growth, imagination, conceptual relationships, and higher-level thinking skills. These activities will encourage conversation and help develop language skills. Students must know that their ideas are important and that their questions will be heard. Have fun and accept all reasonable answers while praising and encouraging questioning from the students.

Vocabulary Expansion

Describe and define these words and phrases:

look up to	vowel sounds	clink your goblets
feeling up to par	chopping block	picky eater
curmudgeon	preheat	mound of dishes
holiday dinner	whatever ails you	cardiac arrest
break a habit	propose a toast	emphysema

Language Expansion Activities

1. Write the menu for your next holiday dinner. Make a list of everyone's favorite foods, and make sure to include something for everyone. Next, make a list of the guests you are inviting. Put both lists in alphabetical order. Use your best handwriting.

2. Make a list of everyone's favorite video games. Rank them according to how many votes each one gets. If you don't like video games, make a list of other kinds of games.

Language Expansion Questions

1. Who came to visit the Marks family? What was the occasion?

2. Why was Pat nagging her grandfather at the beginning of the story? Discuss this question: Is it ever acceptable for a child to correct the behavior of an adult family member?

3. Who else was coming for Thanksgiving dinner? Does your family ever have others join you for special dinners? Explain.

4. Gramps had a bad habit. He had smoked for fifty years. Do you have any bad habits? Are they hard to break? Why?

5. The children loved Gramps's stories and jokes. He was a great storyteller and remembered many things about his boyhood that he shared with his grandchildren. Do you know anyone who is a good storyteller? What are some of your favorite stories?

6. Thanksgiving is a special occasion for most people. Do you remember last Thanksgiving? Where were you?

7. There's a saying that goes, "You can't tell a book by its cover." Mrs. North remarked that Mr. Grunch, who seemed like an old curmudgeon, had been the donor responsible for the rebuilding of the school. Compare what Mrs. North said to the old saying.

8. Mr. Marks proposed a toast at dinner. What does that mean? When do people usually propose toasts?

9. At bedtime, Trish's father always read to her. Who do you think enjoyed the stories more, Trish or her father? What stories would you like to read to someone?

10. What would be a good sequel to this story? Write it.

A SORROWFUL LOSS

UNIT 32

Morphology Concepts

- Suffixes are additional syllables added to the ends of English words.
- **Inflectional** suffixes change words' forms; **derivational** suffixes change words' functions.
- Inflectional suffixes alter words' forms, but not functions. For example:
  - Inflectional endings **-ed**, **-es**, and **-ing** alter verbs' forms.
  - Inflectional endings **-er** and **-est** alter adjectives' forms.
  - Inflectional endings **-s** and **-es** alter nouns' forms.
- Most inflectional suffixes come from Anglo-Saxon.
- Derivational suffixes change words' functions. For example, **-ness** added to an adjective changes the adjective to a noun. (kind=adjective; kindness=noun)

Vocabulary

admission	famous	prosperous	*again*
agreement	fearless	punishment	*against*
arrangements	glamorous	respectable	*friend*
assignments	glorious	sadness	*he'll*
attention	goodness	shortage	*it'll*
careful	graduation	stillness	*I'll*
challenge	happily	teenagers	*she'll*
cheerful	joyousness	temperament	*they'll*
considerate	kindness	tremendous	*we'll*
console	lifelessly	understand	*you'll*
dearest	painlessly	useless	
department	particularly	vigorous	
employment	pavement	wonderful	
encourage	peacefully		
endlessly	pleadingly		

A SORROWFUL LOSS

Story Summary:

During the Thanksgiving holiday, Gramps becomes terribly ill. He has had breathing problems for many years, but has never before been this sick.

 It was a glorious, sunny Friday. The air was clean and crisp. When Tam came over, Pat said, "We'll have to be careful not to make much noise. Gramps is asleep."

Trish was in the den, happily playing video games with Hi. Her dad, who had taken the day off, was reading the paper.

Tam commented, "My little sister plays video games endlessly. Sis is better than any of her friends on our street!"

"But once when she was over here playing, I beat her!" declared Trish.

Pat and Tam grinned at Mr. Marks. Then Pat asked her father, "There's a big sale at two of the department stores downtown. Wouldn't you like to drive us?"

"They'll always ask when I'm reading the paper. Did I ever explain this to you, Mom?" said Herbert Marks to his mother.

"There's a rule in this house: 'Never let your father sit down and read the paper.' "

"Come on, Dad," Pat said pleadingly.

"Would you like to go out for a ride, Mother?" Herbert asked. "Trish, Hi, do you two want to ride with us?"

"Do we have to?" Hi asked. "We were just starting to have fun!"

"Why don't I go see if Gramps is up yet," Pat proposed. "If he's on his way down now, he'll stay with Trish and Hi 'til you and Gram get back, Dad."

Gramps didn't answer when Pat tapped on the door of his bedroom, so she tapped again, "Gramps! Are you dressed yet?"

When there was still no response, Pat yelled downstairs. "Dad! I think you'd better get up here." The tone of her voice said, "Dad, come quickly!"

Herbert opened the door to his father's room. Gramps lay lifelessly in his bed. When he went over to check, Herbert discovered that Gramps had died peacefully in his sleep.

In a quivering voice, Herbert said to Pat,

 "We'll have to break this news to your grandmother as painlessly as possible. I'll start making arrangements. And Pat, you'll have to help me."

A complete stillness filled the room.

It was more than Pat could bear. This gentle, wonderful man. This man whose life was always filled with kindness and goodness. This man who had endlessly toiled for his family. He was her Gramps.

It was Gramps who was always the heart of their family. Just last summer, he had tried to encourage Pat to take over his dairy farm when she grew up. Pat sat down on his bed and sobbed softly to herself.

A few minutes later, she heard voices. "It's a good thing he didn't have a long illness. He looks so restful. It's better when they go swiftly," someone remarked.

Pat shouted angrily, "Who do you think you are? So he wasn't a glamorous or famous person. Maybe he wasn't the most prosperous person. But he was the most cheerful, honest, respectable person who ever lived. He was my Gramps!"

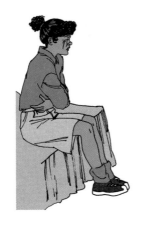 It was useless to try to console her. It was a tremendous loss to the family, but to Pat it seemed personal. She and Gramps had had an agreement. Now he was gone. It felt like her own life had been taken, too.

The day of the funeral was foggy and windy and gray. It seemed as though even the weather understood what a sorrowful loss this was.

The minister spoke about the joyousness they should feel. "He'll be happier," he had said. Pat could hardly pay attention. She kept thinking that in some way, Gramps was still with her.

By the time it was over and people had gathered back at the Markses' house, some of Pat's heavy sadness lifted. Her dearest friend, Kim, said shyly, "Pat, couldn't I do

something? Can't I at least get your assignments from school?"

Pat made an admission to Kim. "I think they'll be mad at me. I mean, I kept thinking about myself and how horribly I was going to miss Gramps. I wasn't even thinking of Dad and Gram and Trish. They adored him, too!"

Standing outside on the pavement, Dad and Gram were telling people good-bye.

Where was Gram's vigorous look? Where was that fearless lady who was Pat's idol since she was a toddler?

Pat raced out to take her place beside them. "I'm sorry, Dad," she whispered.

"We understand, sweetheart," replied Herbert.

Teacher/Parent Pages

Use the following questions to stimulate language growth, imagination, conceptual relationships, and higher-level thinking skills. These activities will encourage conversation and help develop language skills. Students must know that their ideas are important and that their questions will be heard. Have fun and accept all reasonable answers while praising and encouraging questioning from the students.

Vocabulary Expansion

Describe and define these words and phrases:

pay your respects	life support system	against all odds
unwritten rule	funeral home	afterlife
town mall	morgue	make an admission
grieve	make arrangements	take something out of you
die peacefully	heartfelt sorrow	premonition

Language Expansion Activities

1. Gramps died of an illness known as emphysema. This illness is directly related to smoking. Go to the library and look up this word. In your own words, write a paper about the illness and why smoking is so harmful to everyone. Read your paper to students in other classes.

2. Make a NO SMOKING poster. Use a big sheet of cardboard and paint or markers and see who can design the best poster. Display all your posters in the hallway of your school or home.

Language Expansion Questions

1. How did the Friday after Thanksgiving begin in the Markses' home? What was Pat doing? Gram? Gramps? Trish? Dad?

2. Where did Pat and Tam want to go?

3. What did Pat's dad really mean when he told Gram about the rule his daughters had: "Never let your father sit down and read the paper"?

4. When Pat knocked on Gramps's door, there was no answer. Why did she call her dad then? Have you ever had a premonition? Tell all the details.

5. Describe Gramps.

6. Pat said that Gramps was the heart of their family. Do you have anybody like that in your family? Describe the person.

7. When some people came over to pay their respects, Pat heard them saying something she didn't like. She got very mad and shouted at them. She regretted it later. What else can you do if someone says something that you don't agree with?

8. Describe the day of the funeral. Why do storytellers often use the weather conditions to describe situations in their stories? Do you think it is an effective technique? Use it in your next story.

9. Although Gramps was gone, Pat felt he was still with her in some way. What did she mean?

10. The story didn't say how Trish was feeling about the loss of Gramps. She was just seven, but she had feelings of her own. Write a paragraph about how she felt.

MANAGING

UNIT 32

Morphology Concepts

- Suffixes are additional syllables added to the ends of English words.
- **Inflectional** suffixes change words' forms; **derivational** suffixes change words' functions.
- Inflectional suffixes alter words' forms, but not functions. For example:
  - Inflectional endings **-ed**, **-es**, and **-ing** alter verbs' forms.
  - Inflectional endings **-er** and **-est** alter adjectives' forms.
  - Inflectional endings **-s** and **-es** alter nouns' forms.
- Most inflectional suffixes come from Anglo-Saxon.
- Derivational suffixes change words' functions. For example, **-ness** added to an adjective changes the adjective to a noun. (kind=adjective; kindness=noun)

Vocabulary

admission	famous	prosperous	*again*
agreement	fearless	punishment	*against*
arrangements	glamorous	respectable	*friend*
assignments	glorious	sadness	*he'll*
attention	goodness	shortage	*it'll*
careful	graduation	stillness	*I'll*
challenge	happily	teenagers	*she'll*
cheerful	joyousness	temperament	*they'll*
considerate	kindness	tremendous	*we'll*
console	lifelessly	understand	*you'll*
dearest	painlessly	useless	
department	particularly	vigorous	
employment	pavement	wonderful	
encourage	peacefully		
endlessly	pleadingly		

MANAGING

Story Summary:

The Turners have a big family but not much money. Tam Turner needs new cheerleading shoes, but the family needs other, more important things. Tam finally manages to find a way to get the extra money she needs.

Sometimes, Tam felt funny around the other kids. It seemed like they always had plenty to spend when they went shopping. At Tam's house, things were different.

At the Turner home, there was a shortage of almost everything except kids. But somehow, the Turners always managed.

There were six children in the Turner family, and Tam was third in line.

Jack and Liz were teenagers. Jack planned to enter the army after graduation. Liz wanted to go to modeling school. She was the most glamorous girl in her class.

Then there was Sis. Sis was in the second grade, and everybody in the family called her Fearless. Sis wasn't afraid of anything. There wasn't a challenge or a punishment that could keep Sis from trying everything she thought of!

And finally, the twins. Jill and Bill were three now. They needed endless attention, and since both Tam's parents had jobs,  Tam was usually asked to baby-sit. She baby-sat after school, in the evening, and sometimes on weekends.

Sometimes Tam felt that she couldn't manage it. School and family took lots of her time. And now that she had made the cheerleader squad at Tenth Street School, it was harder than ever. Particularly now.

 Tam understood how her mom and dad were always stretching every dollar, adding and subtracting in their

checkbook. But they always managed to make ends meet.

Tam had a problem. She felt fearful about bringing it up, but she had to, didn't she?

 The cheerleaders had picked out some new shoes to go with the uniforms the school provided for them. Each cheerleader was supposed to have the shoes in time for the game on Friday. How was Tam going to ask her mom for cheerleading shoes, when her mom needed new shoes for work?

Everybody thought Tam's mom was the most considerate person in town. And Mrs. Turner managed to find time to help out at school, too. Employment didn't slow her down, nor did her large family.

As her mom drove in the driveway, Tam decided, "It's now or never."

With three bags under her arms, Mrs. Turner yelled cheerfully through the back door, "Anybody home?"

While they put away the groceries, Tam said, "Mom, I have a big problem. I have to ask for your help."

"Of course, dear. What's the matter?" Mrs. Turner replied.

"When I was elected cheerleader, I was speechless. But nobody said we would have to buy shoes to go with the uniform. Now I have to get these shoes before the game on Friday, and I just don't . . . ." Tam started to cry and dashed into the bathroom.

"Tam! Tam! Come on out!" Her mother whispered softly through the door.

 From where she stood, Mrs. Turner could hear Tam sobbing. "Please, Tam. We'll see what we can do. It'll be OK. We'll manage. You'll see!"

"I'm sorry, Mom. I just didn't think. I shouldn't have gone out for cheerleader in the first place," stated Tam, wiping both eyes.

"I have about twenty-five dollars hidden upstairs for an emergency. Would that do it?" asked Mrs. Turner.

"Oh, Mom," Tam said. "I wish it would. But even on sale, the shoes they picked out cost forty-five dollars."

"Tam! Tam!" shouted Jack from the den. "Somebody wants to talk to you. Pick it up in the kitchen, will you? I'm studying in here."

It was Mrs. North. She'd moved into a house down the street two months ago.

"I hope I'm not asking too late, Tam," she said, "but I just found out that Sid has to go to Academic Games practice tonight. He's the math whiz in our family. And I had counted on him to baby-sit for his younger brother, Hi.

"Sid says you have lots of experience baby-sitting, and that you are responsible. So I was wondering. I've got to go back to work tonight, and I'll be late. It will be eleven or so when I get back. If you'd agree to sit with Hi for five hours, I'd pay you twenty dollars." Mrs. North didn't have to wait for an answer.

The Turners had managed once more.

Teacher/Parent Pages

Use the following questions to stimulate language growth, imagination, conceptual relationships, and higher-level thinking skills. These activities will encourage conversation and help develop language skills. Students must know that their ideas are important and that their questions will be heard. Have fun and accept all reasonable answers while praising and encouraging questioning from the students.

Vocabulary Expansion

Describe and define these words and phrases:

financial difficulties	endless attention	it's now or never
shortages	time-poor	on sale
glamorous	stretching every dollar	Academic Games
fearless	budgeting	math whiz
challenge	considerate	family problems

Language Expansion Activities

1. Create a one-month budget for a family. Decide how much total income the family has. Make a list of all the things a family must pay for each month. Make another list of the things a family might like to have each month. Create a pie chart showing how much money is spent on each item. Explain it to the group.

2. Write questions for an Academic Games practice. Have each student in your group create several questions and play the game. See who can write the most creative questions and who can answer the most questions. Have fun.

Language Expansion Questions

1. Why did Tam sometimes feel funny around kids who had lots of money to spend?

2. List the members in Tam's family from youngest to oldest.

3. Tam was a member of a large family. How many people are in your family? Do you think having a large family costs much more than a smaller one? List reasons.

4. What did Tam need for cheerleading? Do you think it was right for the school to expect her to buy her own shoes? Have you ever needed anything that your parents just couldn't afford to get for you? Tell your story.

5. Tam's brother, Jack, was graduating from high school. He planned to go into the army after graduation. What are some other choices students have after graduation? What will you do?

6. Tam's little sister, Sis, was nicknamed Fearless. Why? Do you have a nickname? What are some nicknames of people you know?

7. Tam had lots of jobs around her house. Decide whether or not it's a good idea for kids to do chores. List the pros and cons of doing work for your family.

8. In order of importance, list all of the jobs Tam's mom did.

9. There's an old saying that goes, "If you have an important job to do, give it to someone who is very busy." What does that mean? Why do you think it is or is not true?

10. Predict what would have happened if Tam had not gotten her shoes.

ELMER'S VOICES

UNIT 33

Phonology/Orthography Concepts

- Phonemes for consonant letters **c** and **g**:
  - In a word, the **position** of consonant letters **c** and **g** determines the phonemes they represent.
  - When **c** is followed by **i**, **e**, or **y**, it represents the phoneme /s/.
  - When **g** is followed by **i**, **e**, or **y**, it represents the phoneme /j/.

Vocabulary

accept	citizens	excited	ounce	*cough*
announced	city	face	Pierce	*four*
announcement	civic	fence	place	*ninth*
bicycle	concerned	gently	practice	
bounce	concert	Gerry	raced	
celebrities	cottage	ice	receive	
center	dance	Lucy	recycling	
certain	danger	magic	saucer	
chance	decided	manage	since	
change	excellent	notice	stage	
charge	except	once	voices	

ELMER'S VOICES

Story Summary:

Bud Hopkins and his friends form a rock group, Elmer's Voices. They are entered in a talent show at the Civic Center. Bud disobeys his parents and suffers the consequences.

Lucy Hopkins spilled her coffee into her saucer when Bud announced his plans to be a rock star. Bud's big brother, Nick, played the sax. But Bud hadn't quite reached his ninth birthday!

Bud and Hi North, another student from Ms. Elmer's class, both had excellent voices. They had formed a singing group and named it Elmer's Voices. Since then, they had decided to change the group from two to four singers. Carlos and Dick had accepted places in the group.

Everyone thought they'd be stage stars one day. The city of Jasper would be proud of them. They'd be celebrities!

Scott Larsen was a guitar player who was in

Nick's class. Scott had shown Bud and his group a notice about the talent show at the Civic Center. Once they'd decided to enter, they couldn't think of anything else!

Mrs. Hopkins was upset. How could Bud do better in school when he didn't think of anything except being a rock star?

Hi's mom was making costumes for them. There was practice at the City Civic Center later this morning.

"Mom, I have to go to Hi's," Bud announced. "His mom said if we'd go this morning, she'd finish our costumes."

"Bud, you are spending too much time on this group. You are making bad grades in school. You'll have time for a rock group later!" Mrs. Hopkins's face was red.

"Mom, we have to practice our dance steps on stage at ten o'clock!" Bud insisted.

Just then Pierce Hopkins came into the kitchen. "Lucy," he said, "this is a chance for the boys. Bud's concert is important."

"If we let you go this morning," asked Mrs. Hopkins, "will you promise to finish your reading homework this afternoon?"

"And sometime, I'm going to need some assistance with the fence repairs out back," Mr. Hopkins stated. "You promised me that you'd be around to help out today."

As he raced through the back door, Bud replied, "OK. Sure. I'll be back after practice, and then I'll do that other stuff." But Bud wasn't thinking about those things. He was dreaming of being a rock star.

When the performers were gathered for practice on the City Civic Center stage, the lady in charge made her announcement: "The winner of the talent show will be decided by the citizens. Since Windmill Milk is sponsoring the talent contest, any citizen can vote by cutting windmills from cartons of milk, ice cream, cottage cheese, or any other Windmill product. The winner will be the act with the most windmills."

After practice, Bud, Hi, Dick, and Carlos decided they'd better work on winning. The other groups in the talent show could wait for citizens to vote for them. But that didn't seem like a very good idea to Elmer's Voices.

The boys drew a map of the city. They each took sections and made plans to go from house to house. "Here's what we can do," said Bud. "We'll offer to take their Windmill cartons to the City Recycling Center. And we will recycle them — after we've cut out each and every windmill."

They set off at noon, and planned to meet back at Hi's house at six o'clock.

Mrs. North met the boys as they each returned on their bicycles. "You look like you've had the bounce taken out of you! How about some ice cream?"

They collapsed on the couch. "Ice cream! Yuk!" For the past six hours, they had collected used cartons, cut windmills, and taken the cartons to the recycling center. "No, thank you, Mrs. North," Carlos said. "We just couldn't face any more ice cream right now!" They went in Hi's room to make a list of streets they still had to visit.

Later, Mrs. North came into Hi's room. She said, "Your mom's here, Bud. She's concerned."

Bud had never seen his parents so angry. "Your mother was out looking for you for four hours, Bud," Mr. Hopkins said. "She has had a bad cough, and it took every ounce of energy she had. Do you realize how much worry you caused us?"

Bud felt ashamed. He said, "I'm sorry, Dad. I just didn't think . . . ."

"That's certain," his mother said. "You had homework; you promised to help your dad; you said you'd be home by noon. It is now seven o'clock. No talent show. No singing group. You are one rock star who is put on ice until you finish school. And we will not discuss it any further."

Teacher/Parent Pages

Use the following questions to stimulate language growth, imagination, conceptual relationships, and higher-level thinking skills. These activities will encourage conversation and help develop language skills. Students must know that their ideas are important and that their questions will be heard. Have fun and accept all reasonable answers while praising and encouraging questioning from the students.

Vocabulary Expansion

Describe and define these words and phrases:

unexpected	rehearsal	entry form
pulling in different directions	curfew	one big chance
sponsoring the contest	stage star	musician
red as a beet	celebrities	citizens
audition	City Civic Center	recycling center

Language Expansion Activities

1. Create an hourly time sequence chart of everything Bud did that Saturday. Now create an hourly sequence chart of everything Bud was supposed to do that Saturday. Compare the charts.

2. Create costumes for Elmer's Voices. Draw and write detailed descriptions of the costumes including fabric, color, and decorations. Display your work.

Language Expansion Questions

1. Did Bud really forget he was supposed to come home on Saturday afternoon to do homework and help his dad?

2. Why do parents sometimes argue?

3. Why was Mrs. Hopkins so angry with Bud? Do you think that she could have reacted the way she did because she was so sick? Think of a time when you have been sick and try to remember whether your behavior changed. Describe how you behaved.

4. How many members did Elmer's Voices have in the beginning? How many new members did they select? Why did they do that?

5. Mrs. North was making costumes for the boys. Has anyone ever made a costume for you? Where did you wear it? Compare homemade costumes with costumes you can buy at a store.

6. Bud dreamed of becoming a rock star. What is your dream?

7. Find parts of the story that suggest it was written fairly recently. Why couldn't it have been written ten years ago?

8. Bud's father had asked that Bud come home early and help him with the fence repairs he needed to make. Think of different ways you help your parents. Make a list of them.

9. The performers had to rehearse on stage before the talent show. Imagine what that rehearsal would have been like. Have you ever rehearsed for anything? What was it? Was rehearsing necessary? Why?

10. Did Bud intend to be disobedient? Have you ever done something wrong without intending to? How do you think parents should handle such a situation?

THE PEOPLE'S CHOICE

UNIT 33

Phonology/Orthography Concepts

- Phonemes for consonant letters **c** and **g**:
  - In a word, the **position** of consonant letters **c** and **g** determines the phonemes they represent.
  - When **c** is followed by **i**, **e**, or **y**, it represents the phoneme /s/.
  - When **g** is followed by **i**, **e**, or **y**, it represents the phoneme /j/.

Vocabulary

accept	citizens	excited	ounce	*cough*
announced	city	face	Pierce	*four*
announcement	civic	fence	place	*ninth*
bicycle	concerned	gently	practice	
bounce	concert	Gerry	raced	
celebrities	cottage	ice	receive	
center	dance	Lucy	recycling	
certain	danger	magic	saucer	
chance	decided	manage	since	
change	excellent	notice	stage	
charge	except	once	voices	

THE PEOPLE'S CHOICE

Story Summary:

Elmer's Voices performs on stage at the City Civic Center. People vote for the best act by sending in windmills cut from dairy product cartons. The act that receives the most windmill votes wins the contest. The winners are to be announced later and everyone anxiously awaits the results.

Bud Hopkins and three other boys had formed the singing group, Elmer's Voices. On Saturday, their group had practiced on stage for the city talent contest. But Bud's parents had put his plans on ice.

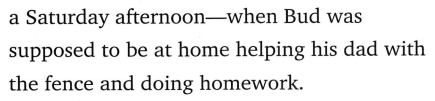

The boys were so excited that they'd begun collecting milk cartons on a Saturday afternoon—when Bud was supposed to be at home helping his dad with the fence and doing homework.

Windmill Milk was sponsoring the talent contest. The winners would be the act to get the most windmill votes. To vote, people sent in windmills cut from cartons of Windmill milk, cottage cheese, ice cream, butter, and other products.

But Bud's parents had decided there'd be no talent contest. Bud was punished.

"I'm not certain about our decision," Pierce Hopkins said to his wife, Lucy.

"No, Pierce. We have to think about Bud. He is doing poorly in reading and may fail. Bud is only in second grade. School is more important than his singing group."

Lucy Hopkins had a terrible cough. By Sunday evening, it was so bad that Doctor Klees put her in the hospital. When Mr. Hopkins returned home that evening, he spoke honestly to his boys. "Your mom is very sick. Her health is in danger."

Bud found a pencil and printed a note: "i luv u. i em sory. i wil tri to doo betr."

The next day, when Lucy read Bud's note from her hospital bed, she and Bud's father understood.

Bud was almost nine. He had repeated the first grade, but he still couldn't read or spell very well. His big brother, Nick, had had the same problem. But Nick didn't get special help until seventh grade.

"With Bud, we won't wait. Maybe he has a learning problem, too," Mr. Hopkins said. "We'll get some help for Bud."

"And Pierce," said Lucy gently, "let's tell Bud we've changed our minds—that he can be in the city talent contest!"

Bud couldn't manage to keep from screaming when he found out. "I've got to get the Voices working on those windmills! They've got to get ready to go on stage!"

On stage at the Civic Center, Elmer's Voices—Bud, Carlos, Dick, and Hi—took their places on center stage. They sang. They danced.

Everyone said they were fantastic! They were the best act by far.

"I wish this contest had judges instead of windmill votes," said Ms. Elmer sadly. "My boys are wonderful. But they won't have a chance. It's certain that the adults will be able to collect more windmills."

The mayor hopped up on the stage to make a speech. "I want to thank those who took part in this talent contest," he said. "The final count of windmill votes will be announced on TV next Wednesday on the six o'clock news. Tune in then to find out who has won the talent contest!"

Wednesday was four days away. And Elmer's Voices still had lots of work to do.

"I'll tell you what, boys," Bud's dad said. "You take two hours after school to finish your homework. Then you can cut out windmills, and I'll drive the cartons to the recycling center. And I'll still have time to visit Bud's mother at the hospital."

By the time Wednesday night arrived, Mr. Hopkins had driven three loads of used milk cartons to the recycling center. And Elmer's Voices had cut out more than 2,000 windmills!

Mr. Hopkins sat beside his wife's hospital bed. She was much better. She'd be coming home tomorrow. But for now, the most

important thing was going to be announced on TV. The six o'clock news had just begun.

Bud, Carlos, Dick, and Hi had gathered at Hi's house to watch. "And now, the news we've waited for. Here's Mayor Cites to announce the city talent contest winner!"

This was it. It was the last of the ninth.

"Good citizens," began Mayor Cites. He rambled on for five minutes. Wouldn't he ever get to the point? At last, he said, "The winners will receive racing bicycles donated by Gerry's Cycle Shop."

"And now, the news we've waited for. With more than ten thousand windmill votes, the winners are Elmer's Voices!"

The boys were excited. They were screaming. "Ten . . . ?" Dick shouted. "I kept a good count. We only had a little more than two thousand windmills."

Mrs. North smiled. "No magic, boys! Other people voted for you, too!"

Teacher/Parent Pages

Use the following questions to stimulate language growth, imagination, conceptual relationships, and higher-level thinking skills. These activities will encourage conversation and help develop language skills. Students must know that their ideas are important and that their questions will be heard. Have fun and accept all reasonable answers while praising and encouraging questioning from the students.

Vocabulary Expansion

Describe and define these words and phrases:

form a group	stay back a grade	last of the ninth
put your plans on ice	learning problem	get to the point
reverse a decision	change of mind	racing bicycle
let the punishment fit the crime	change of heart	keep count
health is in danger	change of pace	at a loss for words

Language Expansion Activities

1. How many windmills did the citizens of Jasper send in to vote for Elmer's Voices? How many windmill votes did the children themselves send in? Write out the word problem in your own words and figure out the answer.

2. Imagine that you are a reporter for the Jasper newspaper. Write out three questions you would ask Elmer's Voices if you interviewed them after they won the talent contest.

Language Expansion Questions

1. Why had Bud's parents put his singing career on ice?

2. Why was Bud's mom so concerned about his schoolwork?

3. Although he was very smart in some areas, Bud had learning problems. He had to stay back in first grade, and he still wasn't reading up to par. Who could help Bud?

4. Is it acceptable to vote for yourself? Who do you think the president voted for?

5. Bud's parents changed their minds about Bud's being in the talent show. Why did they do that? Have your parents ever reversed a decision that they had made concerning you and your activities?

6. Do you think the talent contest winners were selected fairly? Explain your opinion.

7. Bud and his group wanted to be celebrities. What does that mean? Who are your favorite celebrities?

8. A sentence near the end of the story says: "It was the last of the ninth." What does that mean? What did it have to do with Elmer's Voices?

9. Change the story, telling what would have happened if Elmer's Voices had not won the contest.

10. Why did the mayor ramble on for five minutes before he announced the winners? How did that make the Voices feel? What happens when we have to wait to hear an important announcement?

THE CRAWFISH BOIL

UNIT 34

Phonology/Orthography Concepts

- Sound patterns **au** and **aw**
- The sound patterns **au** and **aw** represent the sound in **law**.
    - Use **aw** at the end of a syllable.
    - Or the mid-position if a word ends in **-n** or **-l**.
    - Otherwise, use **au** in the mid-position.

Vocabulary

August	crawfish	haughty	saw	*they're*
aunt	crawl	laundry	straw	*we're*
awful	daughter	law	Tawny	*you're*
awkward	dawdle	lawn	thaw	
awning	dawn	lawyer	yawning	
because	faucet	Paul		
caught	fault	Paula		
cauldron	flawless	pauper		
cause	fraud	paused		

74

THE CRAWFISH
BOIL

Story Summary:

During spring break, Scott Larsen and his family go to
New Orleans to visit their relatives, Uncle Paul and
Aunt Marge. Scott's cousin, Paula, isn't at all as he re-
members her.

Scott Larsen hadn't seen his Uncle Paul and Aunt Marge since he was nine. Their daughter, Paula, was Scott's age. Scott looked forward to seeing them again.

Driving home from the laundry and dry cleaners, Mr. Larsen had taken out the map. "Look it up, Scott," he'd said, "see how far it really is to Louisiana. I've looked forward to this trip since August!"

That was months ago. But spring break came at last, and the Larsen family finally arrived in New Orleans. "It's hot!" Mrs. Larsen exclaimed. "We're not used to such heat in springtime!"

"Thaw out, Mom. Cheer up! Aunt Marge said we should go out back and help her get the lawn ready for the big party tonight." Scott was excited. "Did you hear her ask me to play my guitar?"

Later that morning, someone rapped on the guest room door. "Come in," Scott's mother said cheerfully.

"You're here, so I have to ask if you want to do something." She paused. "But I may as well tell you I have better things to do." The girl in the straw hat had to be Paula. When had she become so haughty?

"Hi, Paula," Scott said. "It's OK. Go ahead with whatever you're doing. We can do something another time while I'm here." He felt like someone had punched him.

After Paula had gone, Scott's mother said, "I think she's the one who needs to thaw out, Scott! Let's go outside."

Aunt Marge and Uncle Paul were setting up a huge awning. "We're expecting a crowd," declared Uncle Paul. "They're looking forward to the crawfish boil!"

"The what?" Scott asked. He'd never heard of a crawfish boil.

"Y'all take a look inside that cauldron over there. We've got two hundred pounds of crawfish ready to boil. When they're done, we'll spread 'em out over these tables, and everybody'll peel 'em and eat 'em! Best thing you'll ever eat!" Uncle Paul grinned.

"I'll tell you what, Scott," Aunt Marge said. "If you can

find Paula, you two could start spreading newspapers on the tables."

At dusk, the lawn looked magical. There were strings of lanterns through the trees, and Aunt Marge's prize-winning garden looked flawless. After they'd met everyone, Scott and his parents sat down with the others to enjoy the crawfish boil.

"Scott," Aunt Marge urged, "will you play that guitar of yours for us?"

As the people were leaving, Paula found Scott. "You think you're hot stuff. Well, you're nothing around here, Mister. You can start picking up this mess. Don't dawdle. Do you expect my mother to clean it up after she's just given you this big party?" Paula was nasty. But Scott was a guest, so he decided not to cause any problems.

Scott went to the backyard and began the huge task. It was dawn when he had finished cleaning up the mess. Uncle Paul came out back and found Scott, slumped in a lawn chair, yawning.

"What are you doing, son? Did you clean up that big mess? Why?"

"We thought you'd gone to bed. This is awful, company doing this work! Aunt Marge and I had planned to clean up this morning!" Uncle Paul had never seen a teenager do so much without being asked.

During breakfast on the patio, Uncle Paul said,

"I'm delighted to have a relative like Scott! I wonder, son. Would you like to come down here during the summer and work in my law office? I'm going to be running for judge, and I need somebody as good as you! I've never seen anything like it in my life!"

Paula's face turned beet red. "But Daddy, you said that I . . . ."

"Never mind, Paula. I've found the person I need. What do you say, Scott?"

Scott was excited to be asked. But the thought of spending the summer in the same house with Paula was too much. "I can't, Uncle Paul. Thanks, but I just can't."

"Why not think about it, Scott?" asked his father. "You've always said you wanted to be a lawyer. This might be your chance of a lifetime!"

Scott couldn't think of a thing to say. Paula glared at him. He felt like he was caught in a net, and there was no way of crawling out.

Teacher/Parent Pages

Use the following questions to stimulate language growth, imagination, conceptual relationships, and higher-level thinking skills. These activities will encourage conversation and help develop language skills. Students must know that their ideas are important and that their questions will be heard. Have fun and accept all reasonable answers while praising and encouraging questioning from the students.

Vocabulary Expansion

Describe and define these words and phrases:

crawfish boil
absence makes the heart grow fonder
anticipation
New Orleans, Louisiana
climate
Southern hospitality
lawn party
haughty

thaw out
cauldron
awning
hot stuff
law office
run for judge
face turned beet red

Language Expansion Activities

1. Draw or paint a picture of how the backyard must have looked at dusk with the strings of lanterns through the trees and Aunt Marge's prize-winning garden. Don't forget the huge cauldron filled with crawfish and the awning. Make a list of all the things the Larsens had to purchase for the party.

2. Go to the library and look up "crawfish." (Sometimes it's spelled *crayfish*.) Find out where they are found and how they are caught. Write a paragraph about crawfish. Have you ever eaten one? What do they taste like?

Language Expansion Questions

1. Where were Scott and his parents going over spring break?

2. Find the paragraph in the story that tells you how the Larsens traveled to New Orleans. Reread it.

3. Why weren't the Larsens used to such hot weather during spring break? What temperatures do you have in the spring?

4. Why was Paula so mean to Scott? Was she spoiled? Jealous? Afraid?

5. What event in the story points out Paula's foolishness? Her demanding Scott to clean up the mess caused Paula's dad to offer Scott the summer job Paula wanted. Has anything you've done ever backfired on you that way? Explain your situation.

6. Create a new ending to the story. Imagine that Scott was not a gentleman. What kinds of things could he have said to Paula? How would you treat a cousin like that? How should you behave if a host treats you that way?

7. Scott had never tasted crawfish, yet he was willing to try it. Have you ever gone to a dinner where you were willing to taste the food even though you might not have tasted it before?

8. Judge whether Paula and Scott could ever be happy together. What things would have to change?

9. Scott was offered the "job of a lifetime," but he turned it down. Why? Has this ever happened to you?

10. Would you like to live in New Orleans? List reasons why or why not.

AN AWKWARD SITUATION

UNIT 34

Phonology/Orthography Concepts

- Sound patterns **au** and **aw**
- The sound patterns **au** and **aw** represent the sound in **law**.
  - Use **aw** at the end of a syllable.
  - Or the mid-position if a word ends in **-n** or **-l**.
  - Otherwise, use **au** in the mid-position.

Vocabulary

August	crawfish	haughty	saw	*they're*
aunt	crawl	laundry	straw	*we're*
awful	daughter	law	Tawny	*you're*
awkward	dawdle	lawn	thaw	
awning	dawn	lawyer	yawning	
because	faucet	Paul		
caught	fault	Paula		
cauldron	flawless	pauper		
cause	fraud	paused		

AN AWKWARD
SITUATION

Story Summary:

While Scott Larsen and his parents are visiting their relatives in Louisiana, Scott's cousin Paula treats him terribly. Her parents never appear to see through her. Paula eventually reveals her true self, but it's still an awkward situation for Scott.

Scott Larsen felt awkward. His cousin Paula was a snob, and she treated him like dirt. But her parents, Aunt Marge and Uncle Paul, treated Scott like a prince.

Now Uncle Paul had offered Scott a summer job at his Louisiana law firm. The thing was, Scott didn't want the job. He was miserable here. He wanted to go home, be with his friends, and practice with their band. It was an awkward situation.

As Scott went outdoors to water Aunt Marge's garden, he overheard his dad say, "We could be settled here before school begins at the end of August."

"Settled!" Uncle Paul replied. Scott saw them shake hands. Did this mean his family was leaving Jasper forever? What about the band they had just formed? What about starting JHS with his gang?

Scott's head was spinning round and round. How could he explain the truth about Paula to his dad? Would anybody ever understand? Did anybody even care?

"Here you are, Scott!" It was Uncle Paul. "Turn that faucet on, will you, son?"

Uncle Paul wouldn't understand why Scott didn't want to spend the summer with the Louisiana branch of the Larsen family, working at Uncle Paul's law firm.

Scott couldn't understand either. How could two people as nice as Uncle Paul and Aunt Marge have a daughter like Paula? It seemed like Paula never got caught. Every bad thing that happened was her fault.

Paula was a fraud. Scott had plenty of cause to tell her parents, but he didn't.

"I'll take Tawny for a walk if you'd like, Aunt Marge," offered Scott. Tawny was Aunt Marge's dog, a big bronze French poodle who thought she was a person.

"Thanks, Scott. Here's her leash. She needs some exercise." Aunt Marge handed Tawny over to Scott. Scott headed for the back gate, but Tawny kept pulling away.

Scott tried to draw the giant bronze  poodle closer, but she yanked the leash away from him and raced off into Aunt Marge's rose garden, digging wildly and scattering dirt everywhere.

"Tawny, quit it!" Scott tried to catch hold of her leash, but he couldn't. Tawny kept just inches out of his reach.

"You ignorant pauper!" Paula was standing at the gate in her new straw hat and white lace dress, screaming at him. "Can't you do anything? You've ruined my mother's garden! Don't you have any sense? I can't believe that you are related to us."

Scott felt terrible.

"Paula!" Aunt Marge was working inside the gazebo, potting plants. She had witnessed Paula's performance.

Instantly, Paula put on her act. "Mother! I was just trying to help Scott catch Tawny," Paula said sweetly. "She's causing us awful problems this morning."

Aunt Marge brushed aside Paula's words. Her face got red. "Someone is causing awful problems, that's certain. But it's not Tawny," declared Aunt Marge angrily. "Paula, you're to go into the den and wait until your father and I arrive." Aunt Marge turned to Scott. "I apologize for my daughter's rudeness."

Aunt Marge marched off to find Uncle Paul. From the backyard, Scott could hear the shouting and the crying. "I'll bet that's the first time that girl ever got caught," commented Scott's father, coming up from behind him.

"Dad, you mean you saw through her? I thought . . . ." Scott was stunned.

"Of course, Scott," Mr. Larsen said. "She's a spoiled girl, but she's your cousin. Try to do whatever you can to make up."

When Paula returned, her voice was like syrup. "I've acted like an awful pill, Scott," she said. "Can you forgive me?" Scott didn't know what to say.

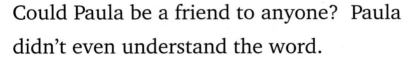

Paula didn't deserve it, but Scott wanted to try to be friends. Could it work out? Could Paula be a friend to anyone? Paula didn't even understand the word.

"Please don't give those roses another thought, Scott," Aunt Marge assured him. "Tawny's dug that garden up many times. I think it airs out the roots or something!"

"Let's sit here on the patio, Scott," his dad said. "Your mother and I have some plans to discuss with you."

Scott wanted to say how he felt, but he couldn't. For his dad, it was an opportunity of a lifetime, but Scott could never be happy here. It was an awkward situation.

Teacher/Parent Pages

Use the following questions to stimulate language growth, imagination, conceptual relationships, and higher-level thinking skills. These activities will encourage conversation and help develop language skills. Students must know that their ideas are important and that their questions will be heard. Have fun and accept all reasonable answers while praising and encouraging questioning from the students.

Vocabulary Expansion

Describe and define these words and phrases:

awkward situation	bronze	true self
witness a performance	gazebo	related
branch of the family	act like a pill	fraud
opportunity of a lifetime	plenty of cause	ignorant
a voice like syrup	French poodle	make it up

Language Expansion Activities

1. Tawny was a poodle. Make a list of the breeds of dogs you can think of. Then, write your own story about a special dog. Try telling your story from the dog's point of view. If you have trouble writing, tell the story into a tape recorder, and then write it down as you listen to it. Share your story with your group.

2. There are certain things about people that make them different. They are called characteristics. Think of all the characteristics that make somebody likeable. List them. Then, list characteristics that make people unlikeable. With your group, make two thorough lists.

Language Expansion Questions

1. Where are the Larsens when the story begins? Why?

2. What had Uncle Paul offered Scott? Why was this causing Scott to feel awkward? Have you ever felt awkward?

3. Aunt Marge was fussy about her garden. Does anyone you know have a garden? What kinds of activities do they do in their garden? How do they feel about it? Why?

4. Offer three reasons why Paula was not a likeable person. Do you know anybody like that? Have you ever tried to make friends with them? What happened?

5. Scott was helping Aunt Marge by taking Tawny for a walk, but Tawny didn't cooperate. Have you ever tried to help someone with that kind of result? How did it make you feel? How did Scott feel?

6. Paula finally got what she deserved. But when she came to apologize to Scott she didn't know what to say. What would you have said to Scott if you had been Paula? Will they ever make up?

7. Compare Scott to Paula. Make a chart that lists their characteristics. Then list your own characteristics and those of some of your friends. How are you alike? How are you different?

8. Decide whether Aunt Marge and Uncle Paul are good parents. Why couldn't they see through Paula?

9. At the end of the story, Scott's dad asked him to sit on the patio for a family chat. What were they going to talk about?

10. What would you have done to help Scott have a better day?

THE BEAUTIFUL, TRUE BLUE GLUE

UNIT 35

Phonology/Orthography Concepts

- The phoneme /oo/ as in **boot** can be represented by **ew**, **ue**, or **ui** (in addition to **oo** [**boot**]).
- Spelling of /oo/ is determined by its position in a word:
  - At the end of a syllable, usually use **-ew**.
  - **-ue** occurs only at the end of a syllable; used less often than **-ew**.
  - **-ui** occurs rarely; it exists in a syllable's mid-position.

Vocabulary

blew	cruise	glue	move	*beautiful*
blue	drew	grew	news	*been*
bruise	due	jewel	prove	*blood*
chew	few	juice	remove	
clue	flew	juicy	screw	
crew	fruit	lose	suit	
			true	

THE BEAUTIFUL, TRUE BLUE GLUE

Story Summary:

Sis wants to give her teacher a gift at the end of the school year, but she doesn't have enough money to buy one. Sis makes a secret plan. Three weeks later, she feels ashamed about what she has done, and when she thinks the others might find out, she is embarrassed and explodes in class. Ms. Elmer understands.

Ms. Elmer had told her class that the day after spring break, they could begin working on their art projects. Carlos was excited because today was his birthday, too.

When someone had a birthday, Ms. Elmer let them bring a treat for the class. Carlos's mom sent cupcakes and fruit juice. Since Carlos's favorite colors were blue and red, Mrs. Corzo put blue icing on the cupcakes. The fruit juice she sent was red.

As the excited students returned from recess, Ms. Elmer said, "You may begin working on your art projects. I'll pass around the cupcakes and juice. Then we'll sing the birthday song for Carlos."

"Is it true, Ms. Elmer?" Sis asked. "At recess the sixth graders said that the second

graders have to go to
school this summer. Don't
we get a vacation?"

"They were teasing
you, Sis. They thought
they were being funny."
Ms. Elmer always made
the children feel better.

Sis thought to herself, "Ms. Elmer is the
best teacher I have ever had! I wish I could
give her some wonderful gift. But what could
it be?" As she sat on her stool at the art
table, Sis had an idea. "If I could sneak some
of these blue cupcakes," she thought, "I

could save them for Ms.
Elmer and give them to
her the last day of school!"

Sis's best pal, Trish,
walked up to the art table.
"Sis," she said, "why do
you have that foolish look

on your face? You look like you have a loose screw!"

"Oh, nothing," replied Sis elusively. "I was just thinking."

"Well, you should get off that stool and look at Bud's art project. It's a diorama with a castle and jousts, like we had in social studies. Everybody says he's the best artist in school, even if he is only eight."

 Watching Bud glue his moat together, Sis's idea grew. She could put a few blue cupcakes in a beautiful jewel box. If she'd glue the top on tight, they'd stay fresh until the last day of school. Ms. Elmer wouldn't remember the cupcakes had been from Carlos's birthday. She'd think Sis had made them by herself.

At last came the final day of school. It was getting hot, a time for summer vacation and trips to the pool. Sis went over to the cabinets under the open windows to find the box she had put there three weeks before.

But the bottoms of the doors were stuck. Blue glue was oozing out. Sis heard Ms. Elmer ask, "OK, class. Who wants to help clean out the cabinets underneath the windows? Are there any volunteers?"

Soon, parents would visit, view the art projects, and pick up their children's report cards. At noon, everyone got to go home. Vacation time was here! But Sis wished time could stand still!

Carlos and Bud spoke up. "We'll clean out the cabinets, Ms. Elmer. It'll just take us a few minutes!"

Sis felt like blood was rushing to her

head. She kept pulling, but the doors wouldn't open. Pushing Sis aside, Carlos said, "Sis, let us in there. We're going to clean out the cabinets for Ms. Elmer."

Sis exploded. "Why do you two always get to do everything? I hate you!"

With tears streaming down her face, Sis fled to the rest room. She'd just wanted to have a nice end-of-year present to give Ms. Elmer. On the last day of class, other kids took gifts to the teacher. But Sis's family had six kids and not much money, so she had nothing to give. "Why did I ever do it?" Sis said to herself. "Now everybody in class will think I'm a big dummy."

A light came on in the girls' rest room. It was Ms. Elmer. "My beautiful Sis! Just look at you! You've gone and gotten your face all streaky, and the parents will be here soon. Let's see what we can do to fix it!"

"Oh, Ms. Elmer!" cried Sis. "I'm so sorry! When it was Carlos's birthday, and we were working on our art projects, I just thought if I took a few of those blue cupcakes . . . ."

"Never mind, Sis. I saw you that day. And I saw your art project—the beautiful jewel box you made to put the cupcakes in. You had a lovely thought, and it's the thought that counts." Ms. Elmer cleaned off Sis's face and gave her a little hug.

"But what about that sticky blue glue?" Sis asked.

"Never mind. The boys will get it up. Besides, it's beautiful true blue glue." They laughed.

Teacher/Parent Pages

Use the following questions to stimulate language growth, imagination, conceptual relationships, and higher-level thinking skills. These activities will encourage conversation and help develop language skills. Students must know that their ideas are important and that their questions will be heard. Have fun and accept all reasonable answers while praising and encouraging questioning from the students.

Vocabulary Expansion

Describe and define these words and phrases:

time stands still	get an idea	oozing out
ashamed	volunteer	joust
castle	moat	a loose screw
social studies	she exploded	jewel box
end-of-year gift	elusive	appropriate

Language Expansion Activities

1. A debate is an argument over an important subject. Debates are planned carefully. Divide your group. Plan a debate about what Sis did. One side should list all the reasons why it was right. The other side should list all the reasons why it was wrong. Then, calmly hold a debate, with each side permitted to speak for just two minutes at a time. At the end, vote to see which side has won the debate. A good debate team can argue for either position.

2. Carlos and Bud were willing to help Ms. Elmer clean the classroom at the end of the year. Hold a discussion about all of the things that need to be done before summer vacation. Make a list of all the tasks. Hang the list in the classroom, and ask the students to volunteer for each task.

Language Expansion Questions

1. What was the cause of the sticky blue glue that kept the cabinets from opening? How did it happen? What did the weather have to do with it?

2. When art projects are judged in contests, how do the judges make their decisions? If you were judging an art contest, what criteria would you use to decide who the winners would be?

3. What did Ms. Elmer think of Sis? How do you know?

4. Who had a birthday at the beginning of the story? What does your class do to help celebrate birthdays?

5. What did Trish mean when she told Sis that she looked like she had a loose screw? When do people usually get this kind of look?

6. Sis wanted to give Ms. Elmer a gift because she had been such a good teacher. Make a list of gifts that Sis could have made for Ms. Elmer that wouldn't have cost anything.

7. The kids were excited because the final day of school had arrived. They were thinking about fun summer activities. What kinds of activities do you like to do in the summer?

8. The children had made some outstanding art projects and were going to display them for their parents. Have you ever made an art project that you would have liked to display? Describe it.

9. Sis told Carlos and Bud that she hated them because they always got to do things for the teacher. Did she really hate them? Why did she say that? Do you ever say things that you don't mean?

10. Why did Ms. Elmer say, "It's the thought that counts"?

MOVING

UNIT 35

Phonology/Orthography Concepts

- The phoneme /oo/ as in **boot** can be represented by **ew**, **ue**, or **ui** (in addition to **oo** [**boot**]).
- Spelling of /oo/ is determined by its position in a word:
  - At the end of a syllable, usually use **-ew**.
  - **-ue** occurs only at the end of a syllable; used less often than **-ew**.
  - **-ui** occurs rarely; it exists in a syllable's mid-position.

Vocabulary

blew	cruise	glue	move	*beautiful*
blue	drew	grew	news	*been*
bruise	due	jewel	prove	*blood*
chew	few	juice	remove	
clue	flew	juicy	screw	
crew	fruit	lose	suit	
			true	

MOVING

Story Summary:

Scott Larsen tells his friends that his family is moving, and everyone feels bad because they are losing a member of their class. But when Scott realizes that the class will go on without him, he begins to feel blue. Later, he realizes what is most important in life.

They were leaving school when he gave them the bad news. Scott Larsen's friends were shocked to hear that his family was moving. "What about our band, Scott?" Nick was despondent.

Scott was the best guitarist in town. He and Nick had started a band this year, and at last, after months of practice, people were asking them to play—for money!

"Gosh, Scott," Pat said sadly, "every year at our class picnic, we'll think about you. Remember at the picnic last year, when you popped a string on your guitar?"

"And when we got in so much trouble for kicking the first graders out of the pond so we could get in?" Tam added.

"And how beautiful the girls looked when it started pouring down rain!" Sam and Al howled with glee. Everyone remembered the fun times they had shared.

"How can you move now? Our class has had so much fun. You can't leave us! Besides, you were supposed to run for class president for next year. Everyone was going to vote for you!" Kim was their class's organizer.

"I can relate to your feelings," Molly sympathized. "I've moved five times since first grade. It's hard to lose your friends and have to make new ones," Molly went on, "but you can do it. When my parents said we were moving here, I thought I could never make any new friends."

"I've got it!" Sid declared. "Maybe we could visit you in New Orleans next year!"

"I'd go," Mat agreed. "Alligators. Swamps. Best food in the South! We could ride the City of New Orleans train!"

"I'd like to go to New Orleans, too," declared Nick. "Jazz."

Soon they were chatting excitedly about  projects they could do to start saving money for their class trip at the end of the next school year.

Scott was feeling left out already. He wouldn't be part of the group anymore. And the thought of having to live near his cousin, Paula, actually made him feel sick.

"See you guys later," Scott said, speeding off hastily on his bike.

As he rode away, Scott couldn't stop the tears that were searing his cheeks. An explosion was going on inside his head. He

could feel it coming. The words and music were dancing around inside his head.

Sometimes when he felt like this, a new song started coming to him. "I should go home and get my guitar," he thought to himself. That was the only thing that would make him feel better now, anyway.

Scott headed for home. At least it would still be home for a little while longer. He remembered their visit to Louisiana a few weeks ago. That was when he'd gotten the first clue they were moving. He'd felt blue ever since. Blue. Blues. *Never Felt More Like Singin' the Blues.*

Scott began to feel better. Now his thoughts were swimming faster. He *did* want to be a musician. And where were the best musicians in the world? New Orleans! There had to be people there who could teach him to play rhythm and blues—and jazz, that wonderful music. Not just play. But to learn to be the best.

His mom and dad were trying to decide what things to put into the garage sale next Saturday. Mrs. Larsen remarked, "Let's get rid of this old green chair. We've had it for fifteen years, and it's plain ratty."

"This chair's not ratty," Scott's dad argued. "This is my good chair. And it's going with me!" He left the room in a huff.

"Hi, Mom! Seems like everybody's uptight," Scott remarked. "What's up?"

"It's just moving," his mom replied. "We've lived in Jasper for fifteen years, and it's hard leaving our friends and our home. So what do you think, Scotty? Could we remove this chair  without Dad seeing us? We could get him a new one for his birthday." His mom looked uncertain.

Scott began to realize how much he loved his mom and dad. They, too, were leaving their home. And as long as they were together—wherever they were—that would be their home. That was what being a family was about.

He gave his mom a big hug. "I love you, Sweetness," he whispered to her.

"What was that for?" his mom inquired suspiciously. "Do you mean that you hate this old chair as much as I do?"

"You make me feel even better than my guitar!" He gave her another hug.

Teacher/Parent Pages

Use the following questions to stimulate language growth, imagination, conceptual relationships, and higher-level thinking skills. These activities will encourage conversation and help develop language skills. Students must know that their ideas are important and that their questions will be heard. Have fun and accept all reasonable answers while praising and encouraging questioning from the students.

Vocabulary Expansion

Describe and define these words and phrases:

had a clue	felt blue	swamp
rhythm and blues	garage sale	despondent
play for money	being a family	amateur
run for president	organizer	searing
plain ratty	suspicious	professional

Language Expansion Activities

1. All his friends called Scott Larsen Scott, but his mom called him Scotty. In one column, make a list of as many names as you can. In another column, list the nickname(s) for each of the real names. See who can make the longest list. (Ideas: Bill-Billy; Susan-Susie)

2. Pretend that you are in the class with Scott's friends. Make some plans for class projects that you could all do together to raise money for the class trip. In pairs of two, be responsible for completely planning one of the projects. Then share your plans with each other.

Language Expansion Questions

1. Scott called his mother Sweetness. Do you have any special names for the people in your family? What are they? How did they get their nicknames? Why did his mother refer to his father as Dad?

2. Explain what Scott meant by this: ". . . as long as they were together—wherever they were—that would be their home . . . ."

3. When his friends started making plans to come and visit him the next year, Scott started feeling left out. Explain why.

4. Why do people often have garage sales when they are moving?

5. Scott's mom and dad had an argument about an old chair. Why did his mother want to get rid of it? Discuss how his father felt. Do you have anything that would be hard for you to part with?

6. When he was feeling blue, Scott managed to find something to look forward to. What was it? Do you think it's possible to find something positive if you look hard enough? What does this saying mean: "Behind every cloud is a silver lining."

7. Scott was the best guitarist in town. Do you or any of your friends play musical instruments? How do you get to be the best?

8. Scott's friends were reminiscing about the good times they had shared. Reminisce with your friends about your good times.

9. The story says that Kim was the class organizer. What does that mean? What are some of the jobs an organizer must do?

10. Predict what Scott will learn from his moving experience.

GRADUATION EXERCISES

UNIT 36

Syllable Concepts

- Review: In a **syllable**, seven different conditions control the vowel phoneme:
    - **Closed syllables** contain short vowel phonemes.
    - **Open syllables** contain long vowel phonemes.
    - In **cvc + e syllables**, the **-e** creates a long vowel phoneme.
    - Vowel **digraphs** create long vowel phonemes, except when **ea** = short /e/.
    - When **-r** follows a vowel, it controls the vowel phoneme.
    - **Diphthong** syllables create different vowel phonemes.
    - The syllable consonant + **-le** represents consonant + **schwa** + /l/.

Vocabulary

audience	graduates	reserved	*only*
auditorium	graduation	responsibility	*says*
backstage	handkerchief	selected	*sure*
chortled	handsome	shimmer	*wind*
circumstance	imagine	tradition	*wolf*
confidentially	Jefferson	ushers	*wore*
determinedly	magical	valedictorian	
entrances	popular	whispered	
exercises	principal		
graders	reception		

GRADUATION EXERCISES

Story Summary:

It is high school graduation night for Jack Turner and Dan Burger. The seventh graders are serving as ushers. It is also time for Mrs. Chung's ninth graders to enter senior high school. All show signs of growing up.

Mr. Miller, the principal of JHS, had asked the seventh graders to serve as ushers at commencement exercises. Sam, Al, Sid, Scott, Pat, Tam, Molly, Mat, and Kim were standing at the auditorium entrances.

After Dan Burger, the valedictorian, made his speech, Kim and Pat would have to rush backstage and slip on the long robes the glee club wore. They were singing tonight. Kim Chung was selected to sing the soprano solo in "You'll Never Walk Alone."

"Remember when we were so upset that we didn't make cheerleading?" Pat reminded Kim. "Now everybody else only wishes they could be in the glee club. My dad says if you wait long enough and try hard enough, something good happens."

"Your dad is so smart, Pat. What happened to you?" Kim loved teasing Pat.

"The boys in our class have never looked so adult before," said Molly. "Has Sam Webster always been so handsome? Only Nick is missing. Where is he?"

"I don't know if he was asked to be an usher," Kim whispered. "Someone said his grades weren't good enough. But Ms. Silver says Nick's doing better. I heard her tell my mom. Only don't say I said so."

"I'm asking Al where Nick is," Molly said determinedly. "He and Nick are best friends." She stalked toward the other entrance. The blue lace dress she wore had a silver shimmer, and Molly looked royal.

"Tam, what's the matter?" Pat asked.

"Why are you so quiet tonight? Is it because your brother is graduating?"

"It's Molly," Kim said. "Tam always did like Nick a lot, and now it sure seems to me that Molly has a thing for Nick."

The lights went down. All the families had been seated, and the JHS band began playing "Pomp and Circumstance." Parents started taking out handkerchiefs.

As the graduates marched up the aisle,

Nick Hopkins slipped in beside Al and Molly. "Hi." His tie wasn't quite straight. But it was the first time anybody had ever seen Nick with a suit

on. "My mom kept fussing over me; that's why I'm so late."

"Says you!" remarked Al. "I bet you were fussing over yourself, getting every hair in place." Mat and Sam chortled.

"Shhh. . . ." Sid hushed them. Mr. Miller was starting his speech. He talked about growing up and responsibility.

When Dan Burger walked to the podium, the audience stood up and cheered. He was the kind of student who was popular with people of every age, a kind of hero.

As they marched out of the JHS auditorium for the last time, the graduates tossed their mortarboards in the air. They hugged each other. Many were teary-eyed.

"I can just imagine how Scott's feeling now," Kim mused. "He's thinking about how he's not going to get to graduate with our class. We should try to make sure he has fun at the reception." The girls agreed to ask Scott to dance.

"Maybe he'll come to the party at my house after the reception," said Tam. "My mom and dad have invited a ton of people. Scott could play his guitar!" Suddenly, her face lit up.

"Confidentially, I think you were mistaken about Tam," Pat whispered to Kim. "The one she's thinking of isn't Nick. It's Scott! That's why she's been in such a funky mood for the last two weeks!"

The graduation reception was held at the Civic Center. This was how Jasper honored its graduates each year. It was a tradition that could be traced back more than 100 years. The Center was decorated in gold and black. There were candles on the tables. It was a magical night.

Sid North was quiet. People thought it was because he was so smart. But Sid was  just reserved. This year, he'd been helping Pat Marks with math. But now, when he wanted to ask her to dance, he couldn't get up the nerve. Pat was the most popular girl in their class. She was in the glee club. She was a gifted athlete. She was funny. She was lovely. Why would she want to dance with him? He decided to forget it.

"Hi, Sid! Want to dance?" It was Pat.

Somehow, her friends were changing. As Kim thought about it, Shantel Jefferson approached her. "Little Chung, you sure sing good. Your mom helped me out a lot this year. Anybody cause you any trouble, just tell me about it. I'll be there. Friends?"

"Anything can happen!" thought Kim.

Teacher/Parent Pages

Use the following questions to stimulate language growth, imagination, conceptual relationships, and higher-level thinking skills. These activities will encourage conversation and help develop language skills. Students must know that their ideas are important and that their questions will be heard. Have fun and accept all reasonable answers while praising and encouraging questioning from the students.

Vocabulary Expansion

Describe and define these words and phrases:

confidential	magical night	valedictorian
funky mood	reserved	soprano solo
honor the graduates	get up the nerve	determinedly
tradition	commencement exercises	stalked
trace back 100 years	mortarboard	royal looking

Language Expansion Activities

1. Ask your music teacher to play or sing the tunes that were mentioned in this book: "Pomp and Circumstance" and "You'll Never Walk Alone." Write down all the feelings you get as you listen to the music. What kinds of things do these traditional tunes remind you of? Have you ever heard them played before? When?

2. Dan Burger was the valedictorian of his class. What does that mean? When he got up to deliver his speech, everybody cheered. What kinds of things do you think Dan said? Write down some of the things you would say if you were to give the graduation speech. Recite your speech for your group.

Language Expansion Questions

1. Why were the seventh graders at the auditorium entrances?

2. Pat and Kim were in the glee club. It took a lot of courage for them to try out for the group. Have you ever tried out for anything or done anything that took a lot of courage? Describe it.

3. Molly said everyone looked so adult. What does that mean? Have you ever looked that way? When? How did you feel?

4. When the band started playing "Pomp and Circumstance," parents got out their handkerchiefs. Why?

5. Dan Burger, the class valedictorian, was a hero. He was the best when it came to grades, sports, volunteering, and helping others. Do you have any heroes? Who are they and why?

6. Why do you think Mr. Miller talked to the graduates about growing up and responsibility? What kinds of things can a graduate do when he or she gets out of school? Do you know a graduate?

7. Graduation day makes people happy and sad. What are some of the reasons for both? Talk about how everyone in Tam's family must have felt when her brother, Jack, walked down the aisle.

8. Pat said something to Tam in confidence. Do you ever tell your friends confidential information? When? Why?

9. There was a tradition in Jasper that could be traced back 100 years. Reread that part and see if you can think of any traditions your school or community has and discuss them.

10. This story discusses the ways people and things change over time. Talk about how you've changed this year.

MR. PRESIDENT

UNIT 36

Syllable Concepts

- Review: In a **syllable**, seven different conditions control the vowel phoneme:
    - **Closed syllables** contain short vowel phonemes.
    - **Open syllables** contain long vowel phonemes.
    - In **cvc + e syllables**, the **-e** creates a long vowel phoneme.
    - Vowel **digraphs** create long vowel phonemes, except when **ea** = short /e/.
    - When **-r** follows a vowel, it controls the vowel phoneme.
    - **Diphthong** syllables create different vowel phonemes.
    - The syllable consonant + **-le** represents consonant + **schwa** + /l/.

Vocabulary

audience	graduates	reserved	*only*
auditorium	graduation	responsibility	*says*
backstage	handkerchief	selected	*sure*
chortled	handsome	shimmer	*wind*
circumstance	imagine	tradition	*wolf*
confidentially	Jefferson	ushers	*wore*
determinedly	magical	valedictorian	
entrances	popular	whispered	
exercises	principal		
graders	reception		

MR. PRESIDENT

Story Summary:

On the last day of school, the seventh graders are to elect class officers for next year. But for some members of the class, concerns about report cards are weighing heavily on their minds. A new student finds friends at Tenth Street School.

On the last day of school, you could always predict what was going to happen. It was the same old thing every year. That is, unless you were Nick Hopkins. On the last day of Nick's seventh grade year, there were surprises in the wind.

The morning began as usual. His little brother, Bud, couldn't find his shoe. Nick had been up late the night before, attending the JHS graduation reception. Now he had overslept, and his mom was nagging him to hurry so she wouldn't be late for work. Nick wondered what it must be like at other people's houses. He was sure it was a lot calmer at Al's house. Al was his best friend, and had been since kindergarten.

 Nick wore his lucky jacket. It was getting hot outside, but he needed it. Even though Mr. Ranson had assured Nick that the report card would be fine, and even though Ms. Silver had said he was passing, the same old worries were there. Nick had had so much trouble in school for so many years that it was hard to believe that he was actually doing well. He had worked hard this year, and he was even starting to think that maybe he could go to college.

Hungrily, Nick wolfed down some cereal and toast. But his mind wasn't on breakfast. He kept wishing he could get the old fears out of his head.

The students had been asked to gather in the cafeteria that morning before school. Their class was to elect class officers, and they would vote before going into the classrooms to get their final report cards.

As he entered the cafeteria, Nick saw Al and Sam sitting with Fernando, the new student, who had only enrolled last week. They called him Nando. He seemed OK, but nobody could figure out why he'd move to a new school with only one week left.

Nick hated being late. "Hey!" he dodged

Sid, carrying a microphone toward the podium at the east end of the cafeteria.

"You'd better find Ms. Silver, Nick. She was looking for you." Sid rushed off.

What had happened? Had he blown it again? It must have been those last exams. Perspiration dripped from his forehead. He felt weak.

He heard his name. Loud. There was Ms. Silver, calling him—in front of the entire cafeteria! "He is the unanimous choice for president of next year's eighth grade class," she was saying. Nick was bewildered. Surely she meant someone else. Now everyone was standing up, clapping. When they started cheering "Nick! Nick! Nick!" he realized there was no mistake. He strode toward Ms. Silver.

Later, he couldn't believe he had actually found the words to accept his new responsibility. He had never been more nervous in his life. He could feel his hands shaking inside his jacket pockets as he gave his acceptance speech in the cafeteria.

"Al says you are a born leader," Ms. Silver had commented, "and I think he understands you quite well."

To top everything off, he had received a certificate for second honors. He'd earned a B average for the semester.

It was amazing how somebody's life could change when other people reached out to help. Nick would never forget how Ms. Silver and Mr. Ranson had helped him.

Years later, when he was a grown man and owned his own business, Nick Hopkins would still look back and wonder what might have happened to him if it hadn't been for those two fine people.

That was why Nick volunteered to do Mr. Ranson's spelling drills with Nando during the summer. Nando had moved several times, and he had problems in school.

As he waited for Nando, Nick heard a noise, but it was only his little brother, Bud, and Bud's new friend, Carlos, banging on the back door on their way to the swimming pool.

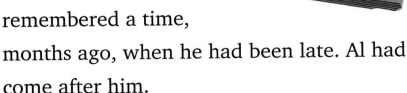

Nick looked at his watch, calculating how late Nando was. Then he remembered a time, months ago, when he had been late. Al had come after him.

Now Nick had to go after Nando.

Nando needed lots of help; his English wasn't great yet. He kept trying to spell words the way he had learned to spell in Spanish. But he was learning. With the help of next year's class president. With the help of Nick.

Teacher/Parent Pages

Use the following questions to stimulate language growth, imagination, conceptual relationships, and higher-level thinking skills. These activities will encourage conversation and help develop language skills. Students must know that their ideas are important and that their questions will be heard. Have fun and accept all reasonable answers while praising and encouraging questioning from the students.

Vocabulary Expansion

Describe and define these words and phrases:

predict	class elections	acceptance speech
same old thing	podium	born leader
surprises in the wind	unanimous choice	B average
nagging	class officers	spelling drills
lucky jacket	bewildered	history repeats itself

Language Expansion Activities

1. Pretend that you are Nick. Write a letter to Ms. Silver or to Mr. Ranson, expressing your gratitude for their help.

2. Find out everything you can about different ways that people vote in different countries. Try to arrange to visit a voting booth so you can learn how it works. Prepare a report on one of these aspects of elections: polls; campaigning; television advertising; voting; campaign promises. Explain why voting is so important in a democratic country.

Language Expansion Questions

1. What qualities did the other students see in Nick that caused them to elect him president of their class?

2. Repeat this saying twice, and then try to explain its meaning. "If you're early, you're wasting your own time. If you're late, you're wasting someone else's time. So always be on time."

3. Explain how Nando feels. If he's entering the eighth grade and doesn't yet know English very well, how do you predict he will do in school next year? Why is it so important for him to get help?

4. What happens at your school on the last day? Do you elect officers? Do you have an awards assembly? Explain.

5. Nick wore his lucky jacket to school. Why? Do you have an article of clothing or a piece of jewelry that is lucky for you?

6. What did Nick say to the group when he accepted the position of class president? What would you say?

7. When Nick got nervous, he perspired and his hands shook inside his jacket pockets. What happens when you get nervous?

8. Ms. Silver and Mr. Ranson had changed Nick's life. Has anyone helped you so much that they changed your life?

9. Explain why Nick volunteered to help Nando with his spelling and English.

10. What are some of the jobs Nick might be asked to do as class president? Would you like to have that job? Why or why not?